"*Born Again* is a book about the redemptive power of the singular voice, arising from the mixture of a multitude of voices, coming together as a single flame to light the way through a landscape of sorrow, evil, extreme beauty, and extreme feeling. The book teeters between definitions of poetry and the essay form to come upon the right way to say the unsayable, telling us things like: 'I am nothing like a tree/ You think I'm in a drought/ You think I'm shriveling up/ You are wrong.' Ivy Johnson is a poet who believes that the I and the spirit are intertwined forever in the act of the poem. She gives the poets of today and tomorrow the permission to gain strength from the force of the persona, with its ability to surround trauma and alchemize it into the sort of language that sustains. Johnson tells us: 'I am free I am free/Believe me I am.' And we do believe she is free. And we believe, in her poems, we are, too."

DOROTHEA LASKY

"*Born Again* is an ecstatic disquisition on the psychic, sensual and cerebral power of religious experience. In a crucible of direct encounter with the Holy Spirit, towering and oppressive mental structures are deranged and reshaped into a dynamic feminist recourse of audacious openings: borderless, raw and alive. Instead of shaming the male god figurehead these lyrics twist in vertiginous funnels disarming power empathically, a rebellious performance that proliferates like quicksilver in a revelatory field of creative fire. Libidinal improvisatory anti-edict, anti-threshold terrestrial tangibility. Expressing volatile, febrile and point blank composure Ivy Johnson redefines (fathoms) what it means to be enthralled as she unburdens the epic weight of judgment and spiritual peril in a veil of viscose corporeality. The erotics of immanence are emancipatory and miraculous here, now."

BRENDA IIJIMA

"Are you 'more Medea than Oedipus'? Are you Jesus? Have you arrived to Ivy Johnson's poetry to experience the revisitation of rape or an abstract 'ecological armageddon' of language or the orifice of a poetic body? Here, we become her wakeful marigolds. We sit across from her like pages of membranes, trying to eat as fast as we can off the hypnotic fluency of her literary fingers, twisting and turning with her as we unlock the 'locomotion of a tautology,' the constant lips and thighs and gurgles or shareholders of her text. And we don't die happily."

VI KHI NAO

BORN AGAIN

IVY JOHNSON

the operating system
brooklyn new york
c.2018

the operating system print//document

BORD AGAID

ISBN: 978-1-946031-23-5
Library of Congress Control Number: 2018943321
copyright © 2018 by Ivy Johnson
edited and designed by Lynne DeSilva-Johnson

For additional questions regarding reproduction, quotation, or to request a pdf for review contact **operator@theoperatingsystem.org**

This text was set in Deutsche Gothic, Gill Sans, Minion, Franchise, and OCR-A Standard.

Books from The Operating System are distributed to the trade by SPD/Small Press Distribution, with ePub and POD via Ingram, with production by Spencer Printing, in Honesdale, PA, in the USA.

Cover Art by Lynne DeSilva-Johnson

The operating system is a member of the Radical Open Access Collective, a community of scholar-led, not-for-profit presses, journals and other open access projects. Now consisting of 40 members, we promote a progressive vision for open publishing in the humanities and social sciences. Learn more at: http://radicaloa.disruptivemedia.org.uk/about/

Your donation makes our publications, platform and programs possible! We <3 You.
bit.ly/growtheoperatingsystem

the operating system
141 Spencer Street #203
Brooklyn, NY 11205
www.theoperatingsystem.org
operator@theoperatingsystem.org

BORN AGAIN

SPEAK OF THE DEVIL AND HE SHALL APPEAR

As documentation encroaches the ghost of emotional dance

I extend beyond the body with strings attached

Dancing with her

I refuse to have my likeness taken

I'm constantly looking in mirrors

That disembodying panopticon

I am the woman of one thousand voices

Of one thousand bodies

In one thousand separate rooms

"And I knew a man—whether in the body or out of the body I cannot tell—God knows— was caught up into paradise and heard unspeakable words which it is not lawful for a man to utter."

2 Corinthians 12: 3-4

OAKLAND, CALIFORNIA

A MAP of THE BODY

I want to write but my mind is somewhere else. I have this thought that I would like to take a dictation device and implant it in my head and have my thoughts automatically downloaded to a hard drive during the ecstasy. I want to appropriate the language from my psychic body and repurpose it for the order of the waking world, an exquisite pulsing corpse. But that's just the thing. During the ecstasy, the elusive, slippery mind. Oh how its scales glint in changing light as it hops from one's hands, splashing into the distant gloaming.

What if I covered every inch of my skin with electrodes and created a virtual map of the body. The image presents itself as a constellation of points, color coded to indicate the different types of energetic production and release, the size of the dot corresponding to the intensity of the energy, a Lite Brite. Like in the way when the slow huff of His hot breath teases my lips and its surrounding skin carmine. His tongue playing to enter my mouth while frolicking in the warm, metallic taste of entering that color. I can feel His psychogenic pigment strike a chord then bleed deep inside the void in my cunt. The alluvial base note of monkish cunt-singing provides a foundation for the whimsy lark of the kiss. Upon the careful entering of His tongue, I can feel the orchestra of every time He's been inside me drone. This is carmine on the key of this map.

IVORY

If I am going to create this virtual map of the body for you I need to start with the ivory, which most accurately can be described as an indifferent light vibrating so rapidly the image takes on mass and appears constant to the blunt eyed, in the way film is a rapid succession of images. Its voice is lush silence. Its particles materialize like ribbons sealed around the body horizontally, the first looping at the crown of my head, the next where spine joins skull, supporting the flailing neck of perpetual infancy. I'm a baby sucking my thumb. Don't shake me. It then loops around where neck meets jawline, as if to taunt choking to an audience gathered round the dumb mind of undifferentiated bliss. Think of death by autoerotic asphyxiation. Don't let it be me. I refuse to jerk off into two dimensional projections. But isn't that eroticism. Isn't that the fantasy. I don't want the fantasy. I want to be cannibalized by god. The erotic is the bastard of Eros.

The ivory charge doesn't play. Perhaps, at least in this moment, I'm relying too much on the flip side of ivory's chaotic violence to paint it for you, like understanding a life through its death. We have a corpse to dissect in some teleologic way. And it's hard to escape the implicit vulnerability of the body as I transcribe it, its precarity when some part is taken out of the world. To experience rapture is to be raped by God, but I give myself over. Still, there's this question of consent. What if I am taken too far. And what of the brutality of a selfhood effaced when two subtle bodies enter the void. As a woman, my life is already expected to be swallowed up into another's. But it's not Him that swallows me. It's the thing that swallows us. This is a hard death to venture back from. He whispers through my tunnel of tears and convulsions, *Lets come back and enter the space. We are in West Oakland. We are in Lobot. We are laying in your bed in your loft. Smell the ginger tea. Touch the hanging plant.* He grabs my hand, but I cannot sensate a way of differentiating our flesh and the terror of this haunts so many of my bodies.

We're out to dinner and I'm back-lit in blue light, head framed by gilded Buddhist deities in some Wes Anderson tableau. In a mawkish display, I take my hair and sweep it over my right shoulder, angling the opposite side of my neck towards Him, lightly brushing it with my hands and meeting His eyes sideways. A spotlight on the thin membranes scarcely masking my jugular. *Does this tableau turn you on?* I ask. I expose one wrist to Him then another. *What about this?* The mood is disassociated, but he laughs it off and I join Him. There is no ignoring the artifice in art, the hand prints on cave walls, that mechanical bird. We're highbrow one moment, debased the next. And maybe my performance of a tableau that expresses adulterated instinct does turn Him on even if it also depresses Him.

IVORY in PRIVATE

To describe ivory is to employ negative philosophy, to describe facticity's purity only in terms of what fact it is not. The ivory buzzes formlessly yet can be harnessed as a type of anchor to be used for reentry into the facticity of material life after undergoing, what has been with Him the not-so-rare sublimity of penetrating the brutalizing splendor of self loss. *I think*, I whisper though seismic trembling, *I think…* and trail off. My tongue can't muscle the acrobatics of words. Not here. This is an actual space and it can't exist without Him.

Ivory as a charge belongs to the Taurus, Virgo, and Capricorn. It is the stability of the four in tarot: the four of wands, pentacles, cups, and swords. This charge sustains always, with or without Him, which is to say, at any given time, there are inuring ribbons of ivory tied under my breasts and around my torso, ribbons composing my wrists, ribbons devising my waist, a charged ivory tusk mining my cunt void, ribbons inventing the fattest part of my thighs, a ribbon constituting each ankle. Since it is ivory light, akin to white, a concentration of all colors, it has been difficult for it to reveal itself to me because of the fact that its long, steady note is first sung when one is conceived. We are born hearing it. Its pitch will warble only under extreme duress. I want to say that the ivory charge ceased when I entered the void with Him but that thought is too terrifying to accept. Before writing that, I asked myself, does the ivory pitch cease after death? In other words, will the world go on without me? Or, perhaps the better question is: how much of that charge is autonomous within me and how much of it is sourced in the elusive mirror of the outside world I watch like a flesh TV? What of this will be teased apart and sunder when I die? Instead of concerning myself with unanswerable questions, I'm trying to teach myself to unearth that charge when I am in the void, to use it as a sort of mountain climber's rope to throw through that spacious chasm and attach to material facticity to pull me back. *Ivy, come back to the room.*

I'm tired. Quiet honestly, I'm exhausted. I go to SFSU a few days a week to teach high schoolers and I have to leave Lobot at 7:30 just to get there on time. On any given night, He and I don't finish fucking for the second or third time until three or four in the morning. We can't stop ourselves. Sometimes the first time is for love mixed with the untempered animal desire of fantasy that has been building all day while we occupy social space. With that out of our system, we go at it again for tenderness, which all too often thrusts us into the Rilkeian vacuity together, that death—what is beauty if not terror. The third time we fuck, then, is a slow and quiet dance to bring us back into the world, back into the world of ivory. If black were a tarot card it would be the magician, a figure full of potentiality, really, number one in the arcanum— the first figure born. In addition, the magician has all four suits at His disposal: two material and two spiritual, and as an alchemist, his character synthesizes all the elements. To describe ivory by its opposite, black, would be to invoke "the nameless arcanum" in the Tarot of Marseille and what most other decks bluntly call death. What else can one call it? I'm on the edge of a tortuous climax that won't satiate. I cum and I'm hungry. I cum and I want to cut my clit off I'm so hungry. I'm fucking dying.

CARMINE

Today I arise from bed after two and a half hours of sleep and float down my loft and out onto Campbell Street all the way to West Oakland Bart, an apparition. I keep looking down to my body to check and make sure that I'm properly clothed and not in my opaque blue nightgown with a v of white lace framing my breasts, nipples blushing pink under chiffon. I'm on Bart and I open my legs and close them. I open them again to get a good view of my crotch to make sure blood and cum aren't slowly seeping though my jeans. There's all this stickiness. My body is scattered, unconfined to its molecular borders, and I'm having a difficult time differentiating between the sweaty vinyl of the seat, the knee of the passenger next to me, and membranes of my thighs, vaginal lips, and ass. I am one with the filth. As I sit, lost in vacuity, secretions of carmine ooze from the wound of my entirety, making a mess of the phenomenal world. How can I find a way to channel the carmine into ivory, the void of death into the stability of the bone charge. I can't do it. My mind is weak. I haven't slept and I'm surrounded by people in the realm of my organism. Some part of me still cums.

Tonight, our fucking is slow. I'm on top for most of it. My hair forms a curtain around His face. His empath's hands are guided by the obscurity of my desire, grazing my back and nipples, brushing against my torso, the O of His mouth and incisors taking one nipple in and out, then the other as I slowly angle my cunt to swallow His cock and pause. This pause drives me wild. I can feel His fullness expand both physically and energetically inside me even as He sleeps. Even as He is elsewhere. Slow vibrational waves seep into my vaginal walls and radiate out to my clit, spilling outward onto the sheets: hot pink. A few years ago, when I was between Brooklyn and Oakland, Brenda wrote me, *All phenomena, all time*. Now I understand that more than I wish to. The bed buzzes with the slough of our amalgamated then singular energy. When He pauses, I don't cum, I crescendo. Our hot pink increases in volume but then deafens in pitch to a terrible base note, the vocal fry of a dying animal. Is this a voice? Is this my voice? Tonight, this is where we stay, somewhere between animal and deity with little to no movement, Frank Ocean playing in the antechambers. I take Him in as deep and fully as possible, feeling the kundalini radiate from where His cock was held snug between my labial lips. The heat of electric pink radiates in loose waves from where His cock is still held inside me, emanating out the center of me like a gloriole as its illumination alchemizes with my skin, trickling down through my parted labia, down His balls, and onto His asshole, hot pink.

SIX DEGREES
of SEPARATION

I am the screaming woman, beside herself
I wipe my menstrual blood over the door of my eviction
I am begging for one more day
I am lost in a place where the prairie is more like a sea
The sea more like a fire
The fire like a distant relative
Speak to me sun
Red mouth of sex
Black tears of death
A fire in the mouth of the river that has dried to mud
I have tried sprinkling the fields in blood
But nothing will grow
Nothing

WHO WILL SAVE US

In the bacchanal I swayed
To the most fashionable of dances
Then went inside the bathroom
And adorned with lipstick the mirror
Everything I need is right here inside me
Target sells that in neon letters
You pay for originality
I am crying out for organics
Deliver me to a presence absent of mind
I want to stage an anti-art ritual where
The sun is real and
Connected by blood
I was once a powerful sorceress
Learned in the ways of magic
To be feared by all
I left totality for
What I do not know
In tragedy
I follow my fate around
And still he leaves me
For a less barbaric woman
If desire is a longing after that
Which inside me I lost

Mimesis is thinking
The difference between the
Real and its rituals
I know it's impossible
But I can remember
A world where life was essence
The soul living through adventures did not know
The torment of seeking
But I know that torment
Yes, that is one thing I know

OUT OF IT

I submerge my body in thick air
I find myself standing on the edge of a cliff
Ornamental and waving from afar
This is what my body looks like
When it lags behind her
I turn my flushed face skyward
It's something like a ritual
My hair turns from blond to brown
My hair turns grey
I am tired of looking in mirrors
I have the ears of a dog
The highest of tones spirals me out
She is with Him
No, she is nowhere
She hears nothing
I can't hear her
I shift my gaze to winter
When I see the void of death
Howling outside my window
She presses her face against the glass
Writing messages in the dew
I don't know her

What is the trace of flesh
What is the ghost of trace
When I leave my apartment
I tell myself I am real
I am real in the street
Then drift up the escalator
To try new clothes upon this real body
This real body that once held a creature
I go to feed this creature and
Nothing but dust
Think nothing of it
Wings are nothing but technology
I float down an elevator made of crystal
The whole thing it's operatic like an aging beauty
Like a white sheet rippling in air
Ophelia floats dead in a river full of flowers and
meaning
Medea smothers her children
Let Maria Callas kill her voice for one song
In slow motion in black and white
The way sound trembles water

THE ACCURSED SHARE

Carcasses litter the prairie like phantom limbs
In a place that was once my ancestral home
A heart beats and buzzes in the clearing
Sky topples over earth with a horizon that cuts
Unraveling the sun sprung all those terrible voices
I am born speaking the language
This rude effigy
I carry the thyrsus
Evoking the name I grew into
Summoning the beyond of cruelty
What else will take me there
I give that you may stay away
I bind you with a name
In the name of Him I bind you
And I bind you good

She left behind the candles burning
Screen door unlatched
On the gravel road the fire of me
Glints and ruptures in the wind
Cows huddle in the west corner of the fence
A sort of prophecy of incubating weather
If you can read it

IT'S A JUNGLE OUT THERE

I am thrown, as they say, into life, perpetually and
Here I stand, reflecting upon
The glowing orb of the present
Tragic and blue
I have trudged up this hill
Retracing my steps from new vantages
A camera circumnavigates my body
As time shifts, a matrix
Shining, epiphanic and reified
Surely I am more Medea than Oedipus
I am a woman
As the roof collapses in flames
I will go on through the lofty spaces of high heaven
Bearing witness, where I ride, that there are no gods
There were missteps in fleeing
For a girl of my age and type
Raving madly in the streets
Singing my banner of freedom
In drink and in fuck
If I had a nickel for every time
Like that time my blood came at the zoo
I was a child
Soliciting wild bloodlust
The hungry animals
Baited by the wafting scent of my cunt
Growling, banging their heads in the menagerie

While living I mask the improper pulsations
I cross my legs
Keep my eyes to the ground
Accumulating to flair up
Like turrets, my sex
I have been told
Zip your self up
Make yourself as small as possible
With men that current
Is scheduled out like telos
Their sexuality unfurling
Is a seed
Incubating inside them
Underground
I am nothing like a tree
You think I'm in a drought
You think I'm shriveling up
You are wrong

ANY FOOL THING

All my life I lay still in bed with my love at my feet
Looking in on me through the tall grass
Stroking His flute in play
Eating and drinking His fill of the finest
I went to the threshold of opal night and returned
Oh world that cannot be
I am wild for you
Wild for your pleasure
I return to the couch and watch TV
I drift and I fade
I bang my head against the wall of my dreams
There is no leaving this place
No, I am a ghost
I am fast asleep
I am layered one thousand times to infinity
The men sleep troubled sleep stirring the house
You could call them my father
You could call them my brother
Oh muse, there should be more words
And everywhere their musk
Their silences filled with poignance
The four is in motion towards the five
My spirit towards earth

When I reach the world
I return to the dandy
He holds a white hyacinth mindlessly
On the edge of human suffering
Returning me to this world
Returning me to this house
I knock on the door
I am here
Hello, I am here

THE WATCHKINS

There are little corporate elves
That stand behind dimensional glass with crayons
Writing operative equations
As they observe a girl sexing with her bare hands
The eyes of the Lord are in every place
The shade at your right hand
The shadow of your mind
Undulates, continuously in orbit
Floating at the rate of exchange
The elves are parodic of my distraction
What is my desire but to collapse
Into the body that produces

In my life I have known death
Before it comes
A voice implanted in my head tells me
I can feel his presence leaving the earth
Hovering behind the real
Is inside me with his mass
Throbbing like the messenger
Implanted in my head
Go back to sleep
That's what he told me
Go back to sleep

OUR LADY of SORROWS

Hunger can burn into power

I have the power of seduction

Men are the head but I am the neck

And I will turn you

Spin your head all the way around

I wear fire red lipstick, I drive a fire corvette

I have the devil behind me and your faith is weak

A wildfire in the woods broke out behind our house

It was born of your sin

Your sex burns so hard the flames strangle you

Night falls and the town's teenage boys pace below my window

Hooting and hollering like wild dogs for my heat

But you are the only one

The only one, the only one

I say nothing

Your wish is the command of me

You look at me and I am born

And it pleases God

I'm so hungry in this world

And this is the only way that I am loved

This dirty little surplus is burning

I rip off the root of my sex and I starve

In ecstasy, in war, and in love

Oh, how the face quickens to a mirror

And empathy slights to parody

Look at me

"And so I tell you,
every kind of sin and slander can be forgiven,
but blasphemy against the Spirit
will not be forgiven."

Matthew 12:31

SEATTLE, WASHINGTON

I'll never be lonely. Loneliness is for the ugly and old. I had a dream I was a hag riding a roller coaster. Someone wanted to take my bones. I wouldn't surrender them. I wanted to spin around. I wanted to contort my excess. People take what they will. Then the dream becomes revenge. Life is lived to spite them.

When I left my town I left for good. Flying over golden waves of grain like a sea holding the quiet. Some pulsing orb buried in amber ripe. Goodbye stillness. I will purge you from my body like the boy who vomits the apple whole with his entrails dangling from his mouth. Or is it the girl who vomits the eye. Look at me now. I want to fall the way Eve fell. The way children bounce on asphalt. And as I grow with age I'll turn it into some comedic art. Look at me now. I look like shit written in lipstick. I will pull myself out of this manhole with my bootstraps thus sayeth the Lord. Where I go there will be protest. Eventually, cars will be aflame and Starbucks windows smashed. But for now, I'm just a girl in the world. Welcome to this tragic kingdom.

When I was growing up Mattel had a slogan: We girls can do anything, right Barbie? Look at her now in this shopping window at Macy's. This is what she looks like buying a coffee on her lunch break. This is the way her hair falls in front of her face as she unlocks her car after dark. This is her pose when she's lost in the night with her shoulder-strap ripped, figure obscured by steam rising up from the manhole. Bring the devil or bring her grace. Fuck, marry, or kill.

I get paid minimum wage to be a hostess on Aurora Ave. When I tell men I work on Aurora they laugh. *Oh, you work on Aurora. That street is known for hookers.* Wink wink. The manager keeps calling me Tiffany. In an effort to connect, she tells me she likes popping her boyfriend's pimples on his back. It's so satisfying. I'm bad at the smiling part. I'm bad at generally pretending. Give me a little smile. If I had a nickel for every time. I'd put them in a pillow case and beat you with them. Beat you to a bloody pulp. And feed that pulp to your children. Keep going. How many will there be today? Right this way. Small talk is the worst bit. These old men were shocked when I hadn't heard of hollandaise. Now they know I'm a village girl. They love to teach me little things.

Steve was a bartender. He was twenty-four, a square white shape, and smoked Marlboro lights. He was about five nine and used to say that maybe if his mom didn't smoke while she was pregnant he'd be taller. Maybe she didn't really love him. He used to talk to me while I washed the windows. There were times I had to bend down and he would stand behind me. I did it like a lady but his gaze reminded me of how the guys in gym class told me their nickname for me was *the virgin slut.* They used to tell me to close my legs. My legs weren't open.

But then it always comes up. There was that time Sarah and I ditched Youth for Christ for a walk around the neighborhood. Spring had just melted the snow into dirty slush. We ran into these older boys with a crotch rocket. They had seen me around school. They had noticed me. As if they had given birth to me. *Get on the crotch rocket, Ivy. I won't take you anywhere. I just want to see you get on it. You would look super sexy.* So I did. Someone took a picture. I was wearing my grey easter skirt and pink easter turtleneck that I had purchased at Deb's with my mom.

A few weeks later my Youth For Christ Pastor took me on a motorcycle ride where we stopped at the vacant parking lot outside of his apartment. It was a few blocks from my house but we were coming from deep inside the prairie. And it's there we would return for the Church-sponsored overnight trip. He had the sluggish body of an athlete given up. He wanted to be the guy with a young blond on the back his bike hanging on for dear life. *Now that you know where I live, you can just walk here anytime.* I never did.

Steve. Steve drove a motorcycle. When I washed the windows he used to tell me about his little sister. How all his friends had a crush on her. He said it was creepy but his face looked proud. How she only ate cereal for dinner. She was a buck ten, a buck fifteen at the most. He would always describe women this way. You know, the blond who's like a buck fifteen.

Steve called me thirty minutes before our first date and explained how plans had changed. I played it cool in this new costume I was wearing. I was trying out sexy and trying out easy-going. It was making my feet hurt. It said I'm intellectual and salt-of-the-earth sexy. I look innocent but deep down I am very bad. It was all true.

By that time I hadn't crashed my car yet so I drove to Lake City. A few months later I would inch my car down his steep driveway covered in ice. It fishtailed to come within inches of crashing into his house. I knew we should have parked on the street but I trusted Steve. *It will be fine.* He was a man so he knew. It was my driving, however, that saved us.

Steve met me outside and walked me into the living room of his house. There were three white guys in their mid twenties gathered around a hookah smoking weed. Two of them were named Brad. One Brad sat in a bean bag chair. When we talked he liked to make me feel stupid. All of them did.

While smoking I told them this story about how a couple of years ago on four twenty I had smoked week out of a gas mask and then rushed to sing a solo for a church talent show. Burning face. Eyes like a skating rink. Singing in front of the crucifix. *Are you ok?* Mom never knew when I was stoned. She only accused me when I was sober and overjoyed. I was just having another one of my panic attacks. I've had them since I can remember. We didn't call them that though. We just said I was nervous like my dad's side.

As I was smoking as I was talking. Yeah. As I was talking and smoking. I started to loose the grip one has over one self. You know. In day to day life. Like how when we wake up we know it is us who are waking up and inside this body we've always had. I lost that. Lacan said ego is a brace. I was all fractured and swelling in different ways. But it was all outside of me. The mirror image speaks independently.

This made it really hard to concentrate on the conversation happening with the Brads. And since I was a ditz by default to them. Well now I'm some crazy girl. Crazy bitch. Whatever happens between Steve and I they'll always know I played the part.

The Brads had voices. Of course they did. And Steve too. But the loudest voice was the one coming from me floating on the ceiling. I had left my body before as an anxious child, rocketing out of the most vulnerable crevices. The violence of it felt familiar. But this time I wasn't protected in the domesticity of it. It's weird how violence can also feel safe. Why is that.

When I tell this to people they think I'm some sort of sage. Like they want me to teach them how to get outside of themselves. How to leave their body behind. I don't know. Google dissociative disorder and browse the potential causes. Pull the trigger. Put your body in a situation of precarity. I've never wanted out of my body. Let me back in, motherfucker.

Remember that scene in Marry Poppins. A man inflated by laughter. Seized and pinned to the ceiling of his den. A stubborn black balloon inside him. A contagion. Ha ha ha ha. He tries to grab the reigns of it. The more we laugh the higher he goes. We're all caught in the feedback loop. It's not the humor of it that takes us. It's how you could go through a wormhole of washing your hands or getting fucked. It starts out nice but then you want it to stop. But it doesn't stop. And the source is inside you. Is laughing on the floor. Come down and have your tea, says Poppins. Rewind. Play. Rewind. Play. Rewind.

Pentecostals laugh. Like during church services they will be rolling on the ground. They call it being slain in the spirit. When you're slain in the spirit you're overcome by laughter, tears, or convulsions of ecstasy. But the Lord works in mysterious ways. I knew a woman who would dance ballet. She was a failed dancer. I knew another man who would run around the room slaying demons that only he saw. He was a failed man.

I wrote this story when I was a child. *A single rose lies in a valley. Her mother told her not to pick the rose. The incline of the valley is too steep and dangerous. Fixated on its beauty, the little girl goes to pick the rose and slips. She lies there lifeless, her body cold.*

God help me.

When doing research for *The Willful Subject*, Sara Ahmed found a Brothers Grimm story similar to mine.

Once upon a time there was a child who was willful, and would not do as her mother wished. For this reason God had no pleasure in her, and let her become ill, and no doctor could do her any good, and in a short time she lay on her death-bed.

When she had been lowered into her grave, and the earth was spread over her, all at once her arm came out again, and stretched upwards, and when they had put it in and spread fresh earth over it, it was all to no purpose, for the arm always came out again. Then the mother herself was obliged to go to the grave, and strike the arm with a rod, and when she had done that, it was drawn in, and then at last the child had rest beneath the ground.

As you read this book, the Grimms' ending becomes mine. The sin of blasphemy will never be forgiven. The book is a restless confession. See my zombie arm reaching out.

I've had a recurrent dream that started in my teenage years. It goes like this. Each year following my birth spring whispers through late winter to the cherry blossom tree in my mother's front yard. When the last membrane of ice breaks from its sheath it seduces the buds out from their quiet to bloom in relaxed opulence. With each year of my life I move closer to the tree as it blooms. Nose arching against the screen door. Toes perched on the porch. Mouth ripe in the grass over roots. Then I am a woman and it invites me in. I relish the eroticism of its ephemeral beauty by lingering under the canopy. The wind shakes loose petals to intoxicate and adorn me. Perfume of life and touch of silk. I close my eyes and am taken.

When I open my eyes I find myself. I find myself levitating three feet above the ground. The breath enlivening my void transmutes from warm to cold. The air around me, condensing ice crystals. Body lifting slowly up and up as its lungs aspirate denser air. Higher. Higher. Terror ringing like the sky is the source of me and I its furnace. I pass beyond the sun into the chilly outer darkness. This is not levitation. This is floating through outer space. Then down. Down. Down.

From the ceiling of Steve's living room I become my own

abuser. The men's voice becomes my own. I ape them and I am cowed. Watch me swing down by my tail. Slaughter me and burn my fat as a prayer. Is this what makes me human.

To be human is to experience many deaths. My body never called me back but I woke up driving home inside of it. It's dark. I'm exhausted. I try and keep my eyes on the road but then I am taken by these clinamen, these swerves on the edge of the city.

A tumbleweed rolls down the highway
Having faith we turn left
Following the sign far yonder
I can't tell the difference between
A sign and a symptom
I conceal an unlit votive within me
Still how they follow
I wake up in a mosaic
I read post-blackout
As a sign from her
With no memory of
My night animal escaping
In another dimension
I walk on glass, I walk on fire
Children wait at my feet
Children perfume my body with oils
They caress my ringlets
Still I yield
I yield to be consumed
By the wild nothing creatures
I yield to die

TAKE ROOT

I am the ugly trailing off soberly breaking edifice
My nerve endings are exposed in warped air like
A tree blown over in this ecological armageddon
As social law becomes habit I'm more or less a lotus eater
Where is the organism to bite me alive
Calm down just have a drink
But what in this wakefulness would happen
Nearing the frequency of absolute reality

Limbs stretch open like a star to speak
God gave me no blood
My blood is the sea let inside
The way seduction opens a thing
The way saltwater is my life
I forgot your human frailty
And drug you to the sunless bottom
You're a doll
I would give you up like birth
But that is not something God will allow
I am not a fish, I am not a phantom
What am I
I can regenerate my entire body
From the most minuscule piece of flesh
I am the one who will take
The world's torture means nothing to me
When I drown I am silent
When I drown I'm ecstatic
It is here that I am born
There are tricks
I have learned from humans
I wring my spine
I cage my mind
I free flesh tangled on bone
And my messiah runs wild

BRING IT

Last night I found myself staring into space outside of
My mother's house lost for God knows when
Suddenly awareness of self was presented to me by the gaze of a man
In a pickup truck down the road carting terror darting towards me
Shot with an arrow and I
The fear moved me like an angry watchdog trapped as
I watched it dangling from a tree by its neck hanging from its leash
My bitch has a pulse
Dares you to try

THE THIRD THING

Lusty blood shed hard on
Impaling clitoris factor
Aimless crying wreckage
Binge drinking happening
Drunken customer service agency
Endless death song searching
24 hour YouTube journey
Buried panic attack bruising
Deep internal wave surfing
Blacked-out violent bottle breaking
Waking bashful mutilation thirst
Morning shame walking
MDMA orgy tiptoeing
Whiskey in bed shame-caving
Looping masturbation phantasms
Spiraling third thing night terrors

THE WORLD IS NOT MY HOME

I have died many deaths
Each time returning my name
A more elaborate metaphor
Stars burn in totality
Let them burn
I want to say my love is ancient
But it is not
I want to say we were born of this yearning
We were not
Love is necessary technology
Tell me what can be saved from his burning touch and
Can you touch it inside me
Please touch it
I am spinning stolen light
I am eating myself like a snake with the tail in his mouth
Burying that shit like a dog and I scratch
It is the animal I worship
I am the snake worshiping
I am my most ancient of kin
I am the parasite worshiping
I already explained
There are no metaphors
Don't mistake them for sickness
And it killed me
I am free I am free
Believe me I am

I fell in at the edge of waking
Paralyzed under decentralized threat
Repenting deep in the vision tunnel
This post-rapture wasteland blasphemy
I saw the four blood moons
As a billboard for his returning
I still worship whatever cruelty
Desecrates the intellectual and get
Sullied one way or another
Transcendence addiction makes you pay
Makes you elbow your way through the shit
And wake up oh so thirsty
I would like to receive a gift
Some sacred animistic lamentation
To blast through my earbuds because
Solipsism is a given and insidious
Like the map in my head
Leading the way to the seers who find me
Flickering the lights
Banging on the piano
Leaving the room oh so cold

SELF CARE PRAYER

Oh, holy-hollow-real
Satiate me with your excess
I can never have enough

BURN THE FAT
FEED THE MUSCLE

Nothing can release
The gurgle of offerings from this fire
As if there were no sky for the smoke to cry in
We roast marshmallows and sing
There is a ceiling to this world
And an altar I have built with my hunger
Which is a fire greater than I
A shareholder of the accursed
We wait to cash in on that energetic torrent
Burning to purge this tainted meat
The end of life can also be the end of power
Dressed in my naturalized mind
I am legion
With no cliff to jump over
I'd rather not die
I'm riding that hunger-strike glow to fade into beauty
The people love it
Fantasies of armageddon as opposed to living

SLIPPERY WHEN WET

Despite exploitation

My desire lingers, free floating

And cavernous, anxiously

Swallowing a hiccup

The shape of a battery

Operated tealight, which forces bloom

Upon the lily billowing

In my throat

I can't breathe

I'm all perfumed with death

Skull filled with flowers

An authentic tableau

Hallowed holy spirit

In my feminist fantasy

I am a severed head

Look at my godforsaken face

As the light slides from my throat

My body condenses the light

I don't need anyone to touch me

To make me real

TAKE a MOMENT
to GATHER YOURSELF

I submerge my hands in ink and smear them across the wall
I cover my body in rich purple paint and rub against white paper
I place a sticker of the Virgin Mary on my bedroom window
next to the fire escape
She hurts with the glow of blue frost
I race down the stairs to make snow angels in the dog-piss
Fill the silhouette of my body with marigolds
Seed the blossoms with tissue paper
and douse them in lighter fluid
I set them on fire and strip off my clothes
I watch the sun set and like Francesca Woodman
I photograph every rendition of myself
With stones in my pockets I am lead to the rooftop
With a voice in my head thinking
Make spiral formations with the rocks
Say the stones will soak up the moonlight
and be used to heal what is broken in me

SIGN

Words punch holes through
The space where events unravel
Every orifice of my body
A signifier of what
On the porch I find solace
In the aleatoric song of the wind chimes
And awaken to my name called across the bending field
How could I be anything
The vulture tipping through stone blue sky
Feathers in my lungs
What is this collage
All the machines at once

I speak of the third thing in the room
Prying voice from owed bones
Cradling a body confronted with transgressions
And bashfully shamed
Oh Lord, I want to be lost in the body of you
I want to frolic through the city like a maenad
I give so that you can give
I was asking for it
Oh holy retribution
I have gotten what I had coming
I will get on my knees and drink your blood, oh Lord
Blood of Christ, refresher of souls
I will be slain in the spirit of you
I will be drunk, oh Lord
Oh Lord, I will be sweet and drunk

CRUELTY FREE

Long fishing wire threaded under the clit and pulled forward
A tugging on the nipple strings
Oh free floating puppeteer
Enter my room and shower me in glitter
How do you manifest yourself in so many places throughout the c
With no strings attached, cute and cruelty-free
I yearn for the nostalgia of your logo
The simplicity of mechanisms yore
How do you have ten thousand fingers always already inside me
The cilia of my lungs
Breathing

FIRST CORINTHIANS THIRTEEN

All phenomena are
Little machines
Cranked up
Clanging their cymbals
For what song
Do we owe this honor
All this time
The fire
On the open prairie
Like a bare neck
On the snow
A body on its knees
Head thrown back
He tells me to grab my ankles
Can you imagine this
My heart might open
My heart may break

NAUSICAA

I stand at the ocean

This tumultuous black mirror

Roaring like life

And reflect

Oh chaos

I am everything

This blood unseen

Trickling out

Pulsing so naturally

But rank in the way

It calls him to me

Yes, the night swarms

In the body of predators

Circling around

This burning ship

For the living know that they will die,
but the dead know nothing, and they have no more reward,
for the memory of them is forgotten.

Ecclesiastes 9:5

NEW YORK, NEW YORK

She is found in the frozen ground of the second layer of heaven. Her coffin is an ice packed mandorla. She is a door. She is a window. She is a cunt. She is the world. Carbon dated to the 5th century before him. Her burial chamber, an entropic death womb. A bowl of coriander seeds. A blossom of cannabis. A platter of dried fur-trout.

Watch me break out and ice-skate the figure eight. I'm dizzied by the world. I keep looping on the ice. Looping and twirling. An inch from her face. I spin and she's a doll. I spin and she's an ice maiden. I spin and she's sleeping. I spin and she's dead.

I would like to put my body there. Again. I would like to relive my trauma. And again. I will smother her body. I will strip my clothes and plant myself on the ice. I will melt the ice between us wth the heat of my spite. Frozen tongues to metal. Crotch stuck on the ground. My warmth will make a hole. Consume the body. Eat your heart out. I want nothing left of her. I get up and twirl myself around. When I gather myself she is gone.

The trouble with writing trauma stories is sublimation. I feel like I'm in the locomotion of a tautology. If I could locate the trauma, a teleology would unfold to explain the why of all of me. Like in a moment of Aristotelian recognition, I would stand at the pinnacle of my suffering, a female-bodied Oedipus who has suddenly realized that she was raped.

There are details. A bouquet of bodega flowers on the top of my fridge. Below the flowers a pack of vanilla wafer cookies on top of a folded card that said I love you and got you a special treat. An empty six pack of beer on the floor next to the futon in the kitchen. The way his naked body seemed infantile. How his baby voice repelled me. The way I never wanted him but had at one time given myself over willingly. A phone call in the morning describing how drunk I was. He insisted on walking me home. I should thank him. He was there to protect me. A flash of running down Grand Street in Brooklyn, screaming *get away from me*. People averted their eyes. I woke up with a black hole in the place of memory. A layer of my body somehow erased. I could have said that I felt raped. I called in sick to Bar Blanc. They were trying to fire me anyway. My best friend came over. We went on a long hungover walk from Bushwick to McCaren Park. From McCaren Park to Greenpoint. To a restaurant where I watched my best friend, Josh, devour a large bloody steak.

By the time Josh and I went our separate ways and I returned to my mattress on the floor of my bedroom, my mind began to flicker. I hold onto my wounds with irascible grief.

And yet, I dream that with enough momentum we can ride that great wind of cruelty into the real, which is to say, pure presence. Touch me and touch me hard; katharos, pure.

Time gets scattered. I'm still asleep in the cold. In violation of my body's will. I hold up the infrared light to my subtle-bodied, naked flesh in the dark room, searching for DNA evidence. Terror is locked in the closet, glowing. I go to the oracle and he laughs manically. Every woman knows her fate. Trauma is a ghost thing. It accumulates so much gravity all phenomena rolls down into its ripple. It's the fourth dimension. The answer to every question. Like how my body was already in the cruel, red light of suffering, buzzing to the beat of something perpetually breaking, outlined in blood. Before him, the year was god-forsaken and the night terrors night after night took the form of a demonic creature hovering above my body, the wellspring of creature fear manifested in a black hole corner of my room.

How years later, lounging on a beach in Santa Monica with Kristen on her king-sized Our Lady of Guadalupe blanket depicting the virgin in a mandorla, she tells me about her rape demon. And I tell her about how years earlier, when I had gone to visit my dad in Nebraska, I woke up with a voice whispering inside my head. And the next day without saying anything about it, my dad tells me that my brother's friend slept in that room a few months before and woke up crying with the same voice whispering in his head.

This trauma thinking, it's magical. The way he's always been behind me, inside me, whispering in my ear, *go back to sleep.* When I speak of the cruel, red light of suffering, I am speaking of the dayglo advertisements that assaulted me each day on my afternoon commute to work. He was already there. I am speaking of the times I was subsumed into my guilt of being female and desiring. From Brooklyn to Tribecca, I transferred from the L at Union Square to the 1,2,3, each day, an Alette walking through the long tunnel. Sneering at the Svea Vodka robot cyborg fantasy. Sneering at the life-size photo-shopped Tori Spelling and her nuclear reality TV show. Sneering at the Terry Richardson Aldo ads depicting anorexic girls licking giant phallic-pink ice-cream cones, to eventually emerge from the underworld to be told that I dropped something. I dropped my fucking smile. He's been with me since before I was born.

When a flicker of the night before began to play out in my mind, I called Josh and he came back to my apartment. He walked thorough the door at looked at me puzzled, asking for details, concluding, *I don't know a man who wouldn't have done that in that situation.*

I was at a complete loss. Backing away from him, my face turned red, than white, then red. All I could say was, *fuck.* Knowing he'd upset me, he gave me a long, apologetic speech, crying tears of haunted empathy, searching for the intersection of personal responsibility and victimhood in my eyes. It was nowhere to be found by him. I tried to speak. I tired to scream through the building. I was a ghost. Grabbing the fragments of what he knew, he deflected the situation into a search for justice, looking up different numbers to rape hotlines, cheering me on to pick up the phone. I called some hospital. A dry voice at the other end reported that I'd need to come in for a rape kit. I asked if that would prove anything if we had had sex before. She sounded annoyed that I was asking such a stupid question. I hung up. I couldn't spare the money for a cab and I sure as hell wasn't about to put my body on a public subway. Josh bought me a drink at the Bushwick Country Club instead. We talked about the distant future. I went back to work the next day and my rapist was there. He was the sous chef at Bar Blanc. His name is Will Sullivan.

When I speak of sneering at the cruel, red light of suffering, I must tell you that the sneer did nothing to protect me from swallowing that dayglo panopticon, as it did not save me from starving myself so I could hollow into perfection. It did not save me from thinking that I had somehow been responsible, that I'd always been responsible, that what had happened was not rape, but something else. It did not save me from picking myself up by my bootstraps to carve myself into nothing. To prove how driven I was, how perfect I was, how I would try my damnedest to be that very image.

Having no story acts as a refusal to submit to the image of the raped woman being a lack of a lack, the raped woman as big black hole, in the corner of a room, sucking life inward to nothingness outlined in blood.

I DON'T SUPPOSE IT MATTERS WHICH WAY WE GO

As if covered in blood
Or red paint from shock
Awakening on the road
As I drained from the loss
The red on the hands
The gold of the field
Not knowing quite yet and
Never quite knowing
The location of this trauma
As if I could march to it in protest

HELL BENT

Everything that happens happens for a reason
I was born a sinner
I have torqued my will
Making myself into the image of idols
I have allowed myself to be worshiped by the needy
Amassing a small sum from their lack
The human will drags guilt behind by its debt
I wasn't a willful child
No, I was obsequious I was on my knees
My neon sex rose up from the silt
Rapt like a laughing gif
Is this what is means to be ravished by God
I have followed my pleasure to the bad way
There is a shadow cast over people like me
When I was a child a woman laid hands on me and prophesied
She said never mind try and follow God anyway
If I am to be cast out wear the robes of Medea
Pronounce banished the Shakespearian way
Your arm covers the black hole of your face as you point towards h
You too know the way

Have you ever seen a New York spring
Chicks hatch and peep as they fall to their deaths
The Bushwick sidewalks are not forgiving
Welcome Spring
Welcome Eternal Return
How can I, too, bloom into empathy
How can I become more than a glimmering dress
Dancing on a rack, drunk and oh so willing
I am detected by no one
Save small animals and children
Come hither, child, come hither

PHANTOM LIMB SYNDROME

The helicopter circles over never waters

How many years have we drifted

Crying out to a nothing

That missing half second

When the brain does not sensate

The pulsing skin

There is no promise of crossing over

In this experiment

A severed corpus callosum

My left hand speaks deaf language

My right hand wipes my shit

Circling the edge of a nothing earth

We come together to tear open the veil

Only to find more phenomena

The age of night stretching

Around our necks

Seeking this passage

In the echoed language of light burning

Many lifetimes ago

In the book of life the sea turns its dark pages
Eggs wash up to shore
After incubating in desert sand
The world evolves to be exhumed by forces
Funded by special interests from above
Some ancient civilizations have traveled to distant galaxies
And upon returning appear as if from the future
Decimated is our world
And time perhaps simultaneous
Phenomena loops while overlapping
Fueled by what machine
In other words
Everything down here does still feel
The fallow fields
Brush the fog's virtual cunt
Over the ticking oilfields
A backdrop for the clothes
I wore when I was alive

I'M JUST A POOR
WAYFARING STRANGER

I have been a hungry waif

I have given my potency to the moneyed

I have begged for it from the other

I have othered the perceived authentic

I have lived among cannibals

The voided center is

A mouth, a cunt, an empty stomach

I dream in ideology

I dream that in the sky is a snake

No, a tornado

It's sucking all the water

Held in its basin

I am the voice of one calling in the desert

And if the devil does tempt me

I will call him the left hand of God

Taking what he has offered

BAPTISM by FIRE

I peel the skin off the air
The spinal extension cord
The heart monitor
The electrical impulses
The social choreography
The natural habitat
The cesspool body
I lift the lid

CORPSE POSE

He teaches me to splay, the master
Like any living creature
Clinging to the edges of the earth
He says
It will hold you
What he means is
You will live forever
This supple prayer
This protean chain of beings
Salvaging their blood in new hosts
The planet earth is going to be recycled
The master taught me
The ancients rendered a natural form
And it is inside him
No it is not him
I tell you, it is not
My ethics are to keep things natural
I paint myself for no one
Seduction is no disguise
There is no theatre in love
I am pure and the master is pure
The truth is easy
What choice do we have in simple fate
I am preparing my body like a child bride
I'll take no pity
The pleasure is all mine
Truly, the pleasure is all mine

He sits on my chest
In hallucinatory sleep
No, it is not a dream
Believe me
I hear a dog whistle
The chosen ones hear
That ethereal slaughter song
Is one steady pitch
Prying the real from
The gloaming of this room
What hovers above my body
Escaping trapdoors to pace
Above my bed like
An alarm clock bomb
What sullied light is born within
Invoking me to be consumed by terror
I am light after all
And petrified by death
The way he tears a sinner
From her earthly body
And captive into what men call hell
You will worship the stone of me
It is buried under the gate
I am not a god, no

I only repent when the night terrors call
With the threat of hell palpable
I find them here inside me
But I want inside them
I will come inside them
With trembling hands
Just watch and you will see

THERE is a LIGHT and IT NEVER GOES OUT

I don't know when I am dead
I never have a memory of it
I have the milky eyes of an old blind dog
But I am not an oracle
The drunken sage whispers in my ear
It's not the future I want
I want to enter the body of the beast
Going on autopilot is different
I give myself over to the puppeteers
Oh god I am Lady Lazarus
Do I terrify
When the light goes out
I put a candle inside
I carve my face into a goofy grin
Can I help you find something

LOVE is TECHNOLOGY

My desire convulses
to be unified with the ritual it performs
which is a type of vague begging
wrists turned toward the sky
blood offerings sealed in the gilded membranes
of baroque goblets, carefully arranged

I want my actions to be
the intrinsically meaningful altar of my body
like how in the epic, nothing
is a metaphor for anything
else, the gods' pending reciprocity
hovers like debt

in this weather I am staying close
to any raw thing I can find in the street
taking cover with Saran wrap
clinging to the fetal corners
of solipsism, the methodologies
one undergoes to seduce the wild nothings

a whole mess of sweaty limbs
loose and wild, lounging on the roof top
after-hours, the human brain can be
reptilian, can fade to white and end
the projected image then applause
our skins remain opulent and empty

we unknowingly watch
our latent desire for communion unfold
perpetually on the edge of a tortuous, phantom climax
the sacral chakra pumping charged air implying
Willhelm Reich, the assumption that orgone
orgasm, organism is another word for god

which is the oily animal of my body
in the seams of Cartesean anxiety
which plays the tune for this flesh to dance to
I want you to whisper the name of my pert little package
over and over rhythmically when I fuck you
given the law that becomes habit

and habit automatic in the habituated body
absent of mind, I want to forget
all my floundering attempts to shut off
the automated mind
partaking in synthesized sacraments and oh
the shame in looking back at a body turned to slop

shovel me up into little plastic ziplocks
while meditating
on the vulnerability implicit in blacked-out
mindlessness for a target
a female body
given the etymological link

of rape and rapture, a carrying off
a snatching away, even the distance of
ecstasy can create the image of one's own body
severed like a trauma, the meat echoes
given the ineluctable modality of time
the edges of containment, I look

to be lost in a single moment

I stand behind the body and bear witness to a fissure I question the history of

I stand in front of the body and shadow-puppet objectivity

I stand in front of the mirror gasping in horror of the other

I layer my mind through the body discovering something like the porous places of an ornate cake housed in a delicatessen window

I reenter the body, experiencing the pins and needles of awakening to a rush of warmth on a bare mattress as I am touched by another after the longest months of a prophylactic winter

I hover above my body lifting higher and higher to a synecdoche source cloud and wax poetic about permanent revolution and paradise now and like Icarus, I crash down to earth

I follow my body swimming like a shadow attached to flesh trying to hear the whale songs but I cannot

I settle into my body to enter the myriad dualities of a closed-eyes meditation

I remove my mind completely and splay a matter of bloody meat on the kitchen counter groomed to be fucked in a hipster misreading of sunyata

I awaken in my body during a cerebral death attack
regulated by shameful amounts of sleep and Netflix

With the slow movement of my wiggling fingers to
wake me I roll to my right side and open my eyes to
live in the body with the thought like a model train
circumnavigating a skinned parameter

GHOST TOWN

The world shifts to the soft tempo of elevator music
Written for the bathroom line at Whole Foods in Union Square
It's ok
I click with the apparition view in Plexiglas-self
Taking a sip of my frap
I slide down a long sterile corridor
And see my reflection spill out into the orchestral street
Catching eyes with the skyscrapers
I mistake my reflection for some empathetic friend
This is what I mean when I talk about parody
The way the mirror mocks me like a sister when I cry
Here come the elves with their high-pitched voice
Specters giggling in florescent light

NOTHING TASTES BETTER
THAN SKINNY FEELS

I'm on the top of the world

I grew up a village girl but now I'm urbane

I used to till the fields

I used to hide my dirty feet from townsfolk

Look at me now

I'm living proof that you can do anything you put your mind to

I used to think I was stuck with this body I was born in

It's this dream I have that I am living

That I am not a ghost

I live in a six floor walkup

The view from my bedroom is a brick wall

The view from my living room is a grid of tiny windows

Eyes of the city only reflect

At night I walk naked to pee under bright lights

Nowhere in this city do I find human touch

The last time I was touched I was raped

Just kidding

The last time I was touched I was raped

By day the womenfolk whisper and look at me

without turning their heads

There's this myth about the human face

I could tell you so many stories

I turn off the lights

The courtyard is locked and filled with garbage

I dream of jumping off

I make a plan

The plan is to fall

I need an implant

I need pills

I need a drink

I need to sweat

I need a job

I need money

I need a filling

I need a trim

I need contacts

I need a doctor

I need a car

I need to live

I need to breathe

I need a vacation

I need insurance

I need probiotics

I need to dance

I need some touch

I need to get out

HOME ON THE RANGE

The way back was consumed by the birds
I'm lost in the thicket of it
Trying to find the exit
By remembering a dream-written song
The prairie grass wind
Is a hovering rush over the field beyond reach
Bending the golden wheat pending export
That we have cultivated in our hunger
In order to obtain money for food
I have been told
It is the nature of my body to sing its enclosure
But my dream sings something else
Beating my fists against my chest
To rupture its open wound upon this world

As if my bare feet
Pierced by the gravel
Is a machine
Productive in the pain
I purchase with my desire
Hunger deferred with a Diet Coke
To walk the city languidly
Like Jesus walked

"Or do you not know that your body
is a temple of the Holy Spirit within you,
whom you have from God?
You are not your own,
for you were bought with a price."

1 Corinthians 6:19-20

DEVIL'S LAKE, NORTH DAKOTA

Saint Teresa of Avila speaks. Her hands pressed to the windows of me. Clawing at the light of Him, cloistered. Her prayer bruises me as she looks out. Rapture is when He comes back for the body. I lay supine in liminal space. What is there left to take. My cup hath runneth over. Desire becomes something other to itself in exhaustion, in raw need. In the interstices of a molten orb, His breath rises. His hooks in me, pulling me under. Pink folds and penumbral light in the cave of me. My hands outstretched towards some unknown calling. Some leap of faith. In the dark room of this arena. An open mouth and its glimmering tongue. A rope around my neck in the throes of Him.

This is my confession. This joyful death agony reaches towards the only facticity and I follow it. It's a kind of truth. Spiritual lust has tormented and haunted me since my sex rose up from below. Being towards death is a picture in the album of this gesture. Desire animates it, puts it in motion. And death, the only proven fact. This beastly giving of oneself completely to the wild nothing. It is that strange force which guides me and I bellow. He, my bridegroom, pulls me by my faltering hand. Within facticity is this thrownness. As if thrown into life by what. Take the picture again. The past is a matrix not chosen. At the same time not utterly binding. The will is scrambled. I harness its fragments and ride with a long black veil obscuring my face. These are my words in the confessional. Hear them and be edified.

I have stepped forward in public display to receive Him. I am ten years old. Donned in itchy white tights and buckle shoes, I stand alone at the altar of Children's Church, hands folded dutifully against my crushed purple velvet dress, face obscured by heavy, wireframe glasses, hair swept back in a K-Mart headband. I bow my head in reverence, waiting.

A crowd of children sit in neat rows of folding chairs at my back as my knees graze the alter in front of me, overlooking a sparsely filled parking lot with freshly plowed snow drifts, taller than angels. A lone station wagon creeps by cautiously on the adjacent icy street. Beyond, the plains roar. Wild wind flurries snow. And what of spring. The sun scrambles through clouds and shines piecemeal in my eyes. Cloistered in my body, it overwhelms to sprout in me, the seed of pleasure buried deep.

The children are summoned to take part in the rite and surround me, each with their trembling arms reaching towards me in the ritual laying upon of hands. The ones who can't reach my body directly touch the children closest to me, forming a web, electric with our prayer, and I begin to melt into a raw, pulsing thing. The perfume of His song fills us. Hot tongues of fire blaze upon my head, spreading an ebullient language gurgling somewhere below. His disciple, a man, takes a small vat of oil out of his jacket pocket, dribbles a glob in his fingers, smears it across my forehead, and as I imbibe Him we shatter. The champagne of Him foams out my mouth, their hands caressing the crown of my emerging form. A pile of elevated meat.

The light now brandished in my face shifts from golden to blue. A tunnel eclipsing all known phenomena. In this place He approaches me, holding in His left hand a golden dart. At the end of its iron tip appears a little fire. With no warning He pierces me. He plunges into me. Rapt in the whole of Him, I dissolve. And when He draws the golden dart out of me completely, He carries off with Him my seed. Our body reverberates as it clings to Him, an amorphous, glimmering blob. This is the first time I spoke the angels' tongue.

Elated and on fire, I return home. Insatiable desire tingling all over my subtle body, glimmering upon my flesh. The following days and months I lay in my bed next to my curio cabinet collection of porcelain dolls and write love poems to Him in a red and pink rose-patterned journal. Unable to sit from the pain of rising ecstasy, I pace around my room. Tearing at the Victorian wallpaper. Standing in the flat blue glow of the refrigerator, the nipples of my unformed breasts taut in the cold. Ravenous for anything to satiate this growing implacable thing, I sprint down the stairs and back up, a feral cat slipping on the linoleum in furious heat. He sees all of time but there I stand, trapped in the horizon, crying out for Him. Each night He sits at the edge of my bed like petulant child with His fingers feathered away at the edge of my feet. At times I think I can feel Him but He taunts me, refusing form. *Forgive me, Lord,* I lament. Winter sloshes into spring and spring into an overripe summer. It is here I find Him again.

Camp Wisagoma is held each year just outside Devil's Lake, North Dakota. Each day of the camp is organized as such—we arise for breakfast, recite pledges and prayers around the American flag, eat lunch of indeterminate slop, attend a solemn bible study, then are released to kayak on the lake, catch frogs or make friendship bracelets, run in three-legged races. Desire builds all morning, intensifying in the afternoon to brim in our bodies into sundown when we enter the sanctuary in our starched Sunday best, single file and contained in the gloaming. Service begins by singing upbeat modern Christian music led by the Praise and Worship leader and His supporting band, equipped with electric guitars, tambourines, and drums. These upbeat tunes seamlessly morph into tearful ballads. This is our seduction of the Holy Spirit.

Toiling through my guilt of failed perfection, I sit through the sermon. One trembling heap in a pile of neat rows. Hungry for His touch. Desirous and paralyzed. My wretchedness blooming, revealed by His words spoken through His disciple. His disciple, the guest preacher, is a strange, oafish man with a gravely voice. The sweaty funk of Him trickles down His face and smolders in His armpits and junk. Our pews quake with his thunderous words. *God sees your sin!* I shift in my seat, trying to fan away the heat of contrition with my hands. *Come to the altar and have your sins washed away by the blood of the Lamb!*

Phenomena floats as the flotsam of primordial goo. Nothing is tethered. The umbilical cord freshly cut, sundered from some nothing thing. I sit at the edge of the pew, gazing at my feet. One brave child arises. Then another. Soon, the altar is flooded, overflowing with children as the band commences softly in the background, playing us with their song. We stand in a long line, single file, shivering in anticipation for the touch of His disciple. Waiting for Him to lay His chosen hands upon us, anointing us in the blood of the Holy Spirit. The gifts of the spirit move in strange and different ways. Some are given the gift of uncontrollable weeping. Some touched are given violent, unstoppable laughter. Some touched are given the most sought-after gift, the gift of heavenly tongues.

In line my quivering body is on the edge of convulsion, salty tears flooding my face, thin snot running down my nose onto my mouth and chin. Electricity rolling outward in waves from my core. When it is my turn to be touched by His disciple, He slowly and gently approaches me, asking me what I seek from The Lord. I unleash an ambulant wail. The slow motion of His hand. Frozen above my head. A ball of white-hot fire, surging in my core. He touches my body. Shocked with the current inside me. He flies to the ground. He stands up, wiping the tears of laughter from his face, gathering Himself to return to me, shaking his head awestruck. Again, His disciple raises His hand above my head. My fire engulfs us. Unable to withstand Him on my feet. I tumble to the ground, immolated. Two acolytes, who stand as men behind me, catch me, easing my fall. They grab a thin, blue blanket and place it over the wreckage of my body still convulsing, legs sporadically opening.

Each morning of camp I arise. My physical body terrorized. My subtle body subsumed in His waning fire. I go to the flagpole to pray. Recite the pledge of allegiance. Eat grey eggs from the mess hall. Kayak to the far shore of the lake. Waiting for the moment the sun eases from the sky so I can return to my cabin to dress myself for Him. Even as I write this my hands begin to tremble, unable to contain the flames of Him, which are licking up my kundalini chakra, extending from my taint as it hisses like a punctured tire out the holes of my face.

ACKNOWLEDGMENTS

Thanks to Lynne DeSilva-Johnson and The Operating System team for their tireless work on this project and dedication to small press publishing.

I would like to offer my deepest gratitude to Brenda Iijima for her mentoring and magnanimous generosity in matters of both poetry and life. Without you, Brenda, I wouldn't have my love, my home, or my book.

Thanks to the love of my life and partner, Jamie Townsend, for their endless love and fire energy that inspires continual growth in me. Jamie, this book wouldn't be what it is today without your keen editorial reflections. You have made me a better person and a better poet.

Thanks to Madison Davis, Joel Gregory, Emji Spero, Cosmo Spinoza, Paul Ebenkamp, Jacob Kahn, and Anne Lesley Selcer for their notes on this manuscript and words of encouragement. Special thanks goes to Dorothea Lasky and Vi Khi Nao for their careful consideration and thoughtful words.

Gratitude to Kate Robinson for collaborating on filming, recording, and performing fragments from this book with me as part of The Third Thing. Thanks to Justin Carder who published a The Third Thing poster with "New York, New York" featured on the back.

Grateful acknowledgment is made to the editors of the following publications in which some of these poems have appeared: *Elderly, 580 Split, Boog City, Open House, The Wanderer, Macaroni Necklace, Apricity, Paradise Now, and Small Po(r)tions.*

Some of these poems appeared in the chapbook *The Third Thing* written in collaboration with Kate Robinson and published by Portable Press at Yo Yo Labs in 2017.

IVY JOHNSON is a poet and performance artist in Oakland, CA. Her book, *As They Fall*, is a collection of 110 notecards for aleatoric ritual and was published by Timeless, Infinite Light in 2013. She is co-founder of The Third Thing, an ecstatic feminist performance art duo. Portable Press at Yo-Yo Labs published their self-titled chapbook, *The Third Thing*, in 2016.

https://ivyjohnsonblog.wordpress.com

POETICS & PROCESS
a CONVERSATION with IVY JOHNSON and
LYNNE DeSILVA-JOHNSON

Greetings comrade! Thank you for talking to us about your process today! Can you introduce yourself, in a way that you would choose?

I am a poet and performance artist in Oakland, CA. My book, *As They Fall,* is a collection of 110 notecards for aleatoric ritual and was published by Timeless, Infinite Light in 2013. I am co-founder of The Third Thing, an ecstatic feminist performance art duo. You can find our self-titled chapbook on Portable Press at Yo-Yo Labs' website.

Why are you a poet/writer/artist/creator?

I started writing poetry as a child as a way of processing both the world around me and my relation to it. For most of my life I haven't felt real; I've felt more like a floating apparition, so writing myself and my experiences in journals helped anchor me to the earth. Writing for me has always been the place where it is imperative to tell the truth, no matter how shameful, blasphemous, or incriminating. I've always been pretty bold in these matters. Growing up immersed in the Bible, I had a deep understanding of metaphor at a very early age. Most of my early journal entries are letters to God and then in my teenage years, they grapple with questions of faith, patriarchy, and the politics of religion, though I didn't have the words to describe that at the time, which led me to poetry. In this way, *Born Again* stays pretty true to my original intentions towards writing.

As a child, I remember thinking that poetry was magical.

Somehow, I could read a poem without understanding it in any concrete way but still have these dynamic emotions stirred up within me. That is ever present. Growing up in an ecstatic religion, I spoke in tongues at an early age, the first experience of which I write about in *Born Again*. When speaking in tongues or bearing witness to another engaging in this spiritual act, I felt changed by the indecipherable words, which according to Pentecostal doctrine is literally the language angels use to communicate with god.

Still, as a child, I questioned the directness of this purported relationship and the motivations behind people's public display of their spiritual gifts. The manipulation of power was and is ever present, even in these seemingly sincere communities. In this sense, poetry has become to me speaking in tongues, but my relationship to language has, of course, become much more complicated as I have grown. I think about the title of a Susan Howe poem, "There Are Not Leaves Enough To Crown To Cover To Crown To Cover". Words have a way of simultaneously delineating and obscuring whatever they attempt to signify with myriad power dynamics playing a significant role. This is why I choose poetry, because the form allows for this slipperiness and simultaneous revolt.

When did you decide you were a poet/writer/artist (and/or: do you feel comfortable calling yourself a poet/writer/artist, what other titles or affiliations do you prefer/feel are more accurate)?

I have called myself a poet since elementary school and really didn't question that until other people that came across my path as an adult looked at me twice for making such a claim since poetry doesn't pay my bills. This has been part of the draw of poetry for me, that it isn't commodified in the way the rest of my life is, beyond escape. I'm a poet because looking back at the choices I made in my early twenties and beyond I have always chosen poetry. I never questioned it. I don't see how it could have gone any other way.

What's a "poet" (or "writer" or "artist") anyway?

It didn't occur to me until a few years ago that I should feel confident in trying out other art forms. For several years I had all these ideas that pushed beyond the page, yet I kept trying to write them. (I'm a Taurus so can take a lot for me to break a routine.) Being an artist means that you'll most likely find many different forms or genres to communicate what needs to be said. Teaming up with Kate Robinson to form The Third Thing, a feminist performance art duo, is what it took for me to finally pursue what had been haunting me for years. If you would like to know more about that experience, you can read an interview we did with Cosmo Spinoza at openhousepoetry. com.

What do you see as your cultural and social role (in the literary / artistic / creative community and beyond)?

I don't think that poetry can effect political change by itself but rather can serve as part of a radical community to confront and challenge systems of oppression. There are books I have read and art I have encountered at times in my life that were the only voices to legitimize my experience of duress under a system that upholds the actions of rape culture as biologically determined and its expression as the test of "true masculinity". This is just one example. Often, it is through the art that we find each other and for the expression of that art that we create safe spaces that push against capitalist modes of economic stability, racism, classism, heteronormitivity, patriarchy, ableism, etc.

Of course, many of us have watched these havens of art and activism become threatened and close down. I was fortunate enough to live in an artist live/work space in Oakland called Lobot Gallery for around three years. We held music shows, art shows, community meetings, poetry readings, sign-making parties, and provided affordable studio/show space for numerous musicians, dancers, poets, activists, visual artists, and the like. In the spring of 2017, after surviving literally having the roof torn off and rebuilt while inhabiting the space, numerous threats from developers disguised as neighbors, and a sixty percent rent increase, we were evicted. After housing a roving art collective for over ten years, the building formerly known as Lobot is now a storage space for Ford Gobikes.

I have said all this without mentioning the immense tragedy that swept DIY scenes across the country but affected the Oakland community in particular. If gentrification and start-up takeover weren't enough, developers disgustingly used Ghost Ship as means to shut down even more warehouse spaces. With all of that said, I personally don't have the answer of how to move forward. What I do know is that these types of spaces are integral to building artistic / activist communities, organizing, strategizing, and fighting systems of oppression. Ted Rees' piece, "Against a Beige Vision" published online at full-stop.net provides a snapshot of Oakland's poetry scene post Ghost Ship.

> This space full of poets, full of people whom I'd marched with, read with, laughed with, argued with, drunkenly caroused with—every single person was aching, and was trying to hold every other person up despite their own ache. I rue the events that led to that moment but will always think of it when I think of what solidarity can look like, what poetry's radical potential can be, and what Oakland is really about: people who will stop at nothing to care for each other while resisting the forces and circumstances of unwavering brutality.

Ted's quote captures what I think the role of artists is in social life. Though I don't think poetry can enact meaningful political change by itself, the solidarity generated amongst these groups of people who are struggling against a beige vision at the least and systems of oppression at the most is what helps keep me alive.

Talk about the process or instinct to move these poems (or your work in general) as independent entities into a body of work. How and why did this happen? Have you had this intention for a while? What encouraged and/or confounded this (or a book, in general) coming together? Was it a struggle?

To be born again is to be ecstatic, to stand beside oneself in fear, rage, or grief (Judith Butler, *Precarious Lives*). It is simultaneously in the body and out of body. It's fucking God, then forming the words with the goo from that encounter. *Born Again* is my bildungsroman. All these themes, the etymological link of rape and rapture with the disembodying effect of consumerism, trauma, heteronormative white patriarchy, could not be separated. Once I got started, I didn't want to stop. I wrote until I felt *Born Again* was complete.

What formal structures or other constrictive practices (if any) do you use in the creation of your work? Have certain teachers or instructive environments, or readings/writings/work of other creative people informed the way you work/write?

When reading Saint Teresa of Avila I was struck that she was writing a confessional. As a young poet in the literary world, the word confessional meant domestic, melodramatic, pedestrian, and wreaked of the so-called insipid thoughts of teenage girls. To be called "confessional" in a workshop was the ultimate embarrassment. In my early twenties and on into graduate school, my writing suffered as a result of this taboo upheld by dude culture in the literary scene. There are several books that helped me to personally debunk this misogynistic attitude towards confessional, or personal writing.

I hold many debts to these writers of the books who went on to influence me to write *Born Again*, though I don't consider my book or the following a list of confessional writing per se. Some of these books include *The Fast* by Hannah Wieners, *Killing Kanoko* by Hiromi Ito, *Rome* by Dorothea Lasky, *Marjorie Kempe* by Robert Gluck, *Early Linoleum* by Brenda Iijima, *Sabor Ami* by Cecilia Vicuna and selected works by

Wendy Trevino.

While writing *Born Again* I also felt myself returning again and again to Passolini's *Medea*, thinking of Medea's disconnection from her grandfather, Helios, and concomitantly her powers of sorcery, as a way to parse Luckas' ideas about modernity (*The Theory of the Novel*). He writes of how the novel expresses a break from the epic where the hero's meaning is intrinsic to their action "because the soul rests within itself even as it acts" (29). In modernity we have literary characters whose plight is a rift between inside and outside, a separation of self from any intrinsic home. "Philosophy is really homesickness," (as cited in Luckas, 29). As a lapsed Pentecostal and as one who could speak in the tongues of men and of angels, I greatly identify with Medea in the moment after she has killed her brother, stolen the golden fleece, and while fleeing with Jason and the Argonauts she screams, "Speak to me earth! I can no longer hear your voice!" In this sense, *Born Again* is much more than a separation from God; it's primordial desire.

"New York, New York," [p. 63] was used in various performances and video art created by The Third Thing. This lyric essay both informed and was informed by the images and performances created.

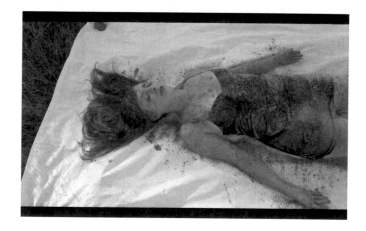

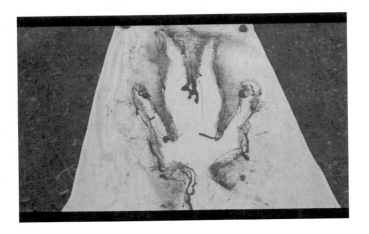

These images are screen shots from video filmed in Tilden Regional Park in Oakland, CA in the summer of 2014 by The Third Thing. They were projected as part of performances for the Under the Influence Reading Series at The Emerald Tablet in San Fransisco in 2014, Poet's Theatre at Omni Commons in 2015, also in San Fransisco, and for "Blood Ritual," both a performance and month-long art installation at E.M Wolfman, in Oakland, CA, in 2015.

WHY PRINT / DOCUMENT?

The Operating System uses the language "print document" to differentiate from the book-object as part of our mission to distinguish the act of documentation-in-book-FORM from the act of publishing as a backwards-facing replication of the book's agentive *role* as it may have appeared the last several centuries of its history. Ultimately, I approach the book as TECHNOLOGY: one of a variety of printed documents (in this case, bound*) that humans have invented and in turn used to archive and disseminate ideas, beliefs, stories, and other evidence of production*

Ownership and use of printing presses and access to (or restriction of printed materials) has long been a site of struggle, related in many ways to revolutionary activity and the fight for civil rights and free speech all over the world. While (in many countries) the contemporary quotidian landscape has indeed drastically shifted in its access to platforms for sharing information and in the widespread ability to "publish" digitally, even with extremely limited resources, the importance of publication on physical media has not diminished. In fact, this may be the most critical time in recent history for activist groups, artists, and others to insist upon learning, establishing, and encouraging personal and community documentation practices. Hear me out.

With The OS's print endeavors I wanted to open up a conversation about this: the ultimately radical, transgressive act of creating PRINT /DOCUMENTATION in the digital age. It's a question of the archive, and of history: who gets to tell the story, and what evidence of our life, our behaviors, our experiences are we leaving behind? We can know little to nothing about the future into which we're leaving an unprecedentedly digital document trail — but we can be assured that publications, government agencies, museums, schools, and other institutional powers that be will continue to leave BOTH a digital and print version of their production for the official record. Will we?

As a (rogue) anthropologist and long time academic, I can easily pull up many accounts about how lives, behaviors, experiences — how THE STORY of a time or place — was pieced together using the deep study of correspondence, notebooks, and other physical documents which are no longer the norm in many lives and practices. As we move our creative behaviors towards digital note taking, and even audio and video, what can we predict about future technology that is in any way assuring that our stories will be accurately told – or told at all? How will we leave these things for the record?

In these documents we say:
WE WERE HERE, WE EXISTED, WE HAVE A DIFFERENT STORY

- Lynne DeSilva-Johnson, Founder/Creative Director
THE OPERATING SYSTEM, Brooklyn NY 2018

Ark Hive-Marthe Reed [2019]

A Bony Framework for the Tangible Universe-D. Allen [kin(d)*, 2019]

Śnienie / Dreaming - Marta Zelwan/Krystyna Sakowicz, (Polish-English/dual-language) trans. Victoria Miluch [glossarium, 2019]

Opera on TV-James Brunton [kin(d)*, 2019]

aregho: Pareil-À-Rien / Alparegho, Like Nothing Else - Hélène Sanguinetti ench-English/dual-language), trans. Ann Cefola [glossarium, 2019]

Hall of Waters-Berry Grass [kin(d)*, 2019]

High Tide Of The Eyes - Bijan Elahi (Farsi-English/dual-language) as. Rebecca Ruth Gould and Kayvan Tahmasebian [glossarium, 2019]

ade for You a New Machine and All it Does is Hope - Richard Lucyshyn [2019]

Illusory Borders-Heidi Reszies [2019]

Transitional Object-Adrian Silbernagel [kin(d)*, 2019]

A Year of Misreading the Wildcats [2019]

Absence So Great and Spontaneous It Is Evidence of Light - Anne Gorrick [2018]

The Book of Everyday Instruction - Chloe Bass [2018]

Executive Orders Vol. II - a collaboration with the Organism for Poetic Research [2018]

One More Revolution - Andrea Mazzariello [2018]

The Suitcase Tree - Filip Marinovich [2018]

Chlorosis - Michael Flatt and Derrick Mund [2018]

Sussuros a Mi Padre - Erick Sáenz [2018]

Sharing Plastic - Blake Nemec [2018]

e Book of Sounds - Mehdi Navid (Farsi dual language, trans. Tina Rahimi) [2018]

Corpore Sano : Creative Practice and the Challenged Body [Anthology, 2018]; Lynne DeSilva-Johnson and Jay Besemer, co-editors

Abandoners - Lesley Ann Wheeler [2018]

Jazzercise is a Language - Gabriel Ojeda-Sague [2018]

Return Trip / Viaje Al Regreso - Israel Dominguez; (Spanish-English dual language) trans. Margaret Randall [2018]

Born Again - Ivy Johnson [2018]

Attendance - Rocío Carlos and Rachel McLeod Kaminer [2018]

Singing for Nothing - Wally Swist [2018]

The Ways of the Monster - Jay Besemer [2018]

Walking Away From Explosions in Slow Motion - Gregory Crosby [2018]

The Unspoken - Bob Holman [Bowery Books imprint - 2018]

Field Guide to Autobiography - Melissa Eleftherion [2018]

Kawsay: The Flame of the Jungle - María Vázquez Valdez (Spanish-English dual language) trans. Margaret Randall [2018]

DOC U MENT
/däkyəmənt/

First meant "instruction" or "evidence," whether written or not.

noun - a piece of written, printed, or electronic matter that provides information or evidence or that serves as an official record
verb - record (something) in written, photographic, or other form
synonyms - paper - deed - record - writing - act - instrument

[*Middle English, precept, from Old French, from Latin documentum, example, proof, from docre, to teach; see dek- in Indo-European roots.*]

Who is responsible for the manufacture of value?

Based on what supercilious ontology have we landed in a space where we vie against other creative people in vain pursuit of the fleeting credibilities of the scarcity economy, rather than freely collaborating and sharing openly with each other in ecstatic celebration of MAKING?

While we understand and acknowledge the economic pressures and fear-mongering that threatens to dominate and crush the creative impulse, we also believe that ***now more than ever we have the tools to relinquish agency via cooperative means,*** fueled by the fires of the Open Source Movement.

Looking out across the invisible vistas of that rhizomatic parallel country we can begin to see our community beyond constraints, in the place where intention meets resilient, proactive, collaborative organization.

Here is a document born of that belief, sown purely of imagination and will. When we document we assert. We print to make real, to reify our being there.When we do so with mindful intention to address our process, to open our work to others, to create beauty in words in space, to respect and acknowledge the strength of the page we now hold physical, a thing in our hand... we remind ourselves that, like Dorothy: *we had the power all along, my dears.*

THE PRINT! DOCUMENT SERIES

is a project of
the trouble with bartleby
in collaboration with
the operating system